1.

Engineering and Science
University Magnet School
imagine, investigate, invent

ESUMS Mission Statement:

Engineering and Science University Magnet School, a public college preparatory middle and high school, challenges students to imagine, investigate, and invent while preparing them for demanding STEM programs at the collegiate level.

About ESUMS:

The Engineering and Science University Magnet School, or ESUMS, was opened in 2008. It was created with a very special purpose: to educate and train the next generation of engineers, scientists, and leaders. ESUMS has maintained high standards since its opening, and students are set up for success with advanced courses in math and science. Students are accepted based on entry into a lottery, and class sizes are under 100 students. ESUMS holds a very diverse student body, with students from many towns around the New Haven area.

ESUMS Website: www.esumsnewhaven.com

© Daniel Molster

Introduction to Lines & Sketching

© 2013, Daniel Molster
daniel.molster@gmail.com

ALL RIGHTS RESERVED. This book contains material protected under International and Federal Copyright Laws and Treaties. Any unauthorized reprint or use of this material is prohibited. No part of this book may be reproduced or transmitted in any form or by any means, electronic or mechanical, including photocopying, recording, or by any information storage and retrieval system without express written permission from the author / publisher.

Printed in the U.S.A.

First Edition

Table of Contents

Forward: What is Engineering?

Part 1: Line Conventions & Lines

1. What is a Line Convention?
2. Many Types of Lines
3. Center Lines
4. Construction Lines
5. Dimension Lines
6. Extension Lines
7. Hidden Lines
8. Leader Lines
9. Long-Break Lines
10. Object Lines
11. Projection Lines
12. Section Lines
13. Short-Break Lines

Part 2: Sketching

14. What is Sketching?

15. Sketching and Lines Are a Perfect Pair

16. Cabinet Pictorial

17. Cavalier Pictorial

18. Cabinet VS. Cavalier Pictorials

19. The Basics of Sketching: Four Major Views

20. One-Point Perspective: What's it All About?

21. Two-Point Perspective: A Fresh Look

22. Where to Next: A Reflection of Your Work

Part 3: Test Your Knowledge

Forward

The book you are about to read was written by a high-school student. That's right, this very book you hold in your hands (or in your digital hands if using an E-Reader) was written by a high-school I.E.D. student at the Engineering and Science University Magnet School (or ESUMS for short). But before we get into the book, what exactly IS I.E.D.? I.E.D. stands for Introduction to Engineering Design, which is a course designed by Project Lead The Way (PLTW, for short). But what exactly is engineering about? I.E.D., for example is about Geometry, Sketching, C.A.D. (Computer Aided Drawing/Drafting/Design), Being Creative, and Critical Thinking.

Critical Thinking is hard to put into words. My definition of Critical Thinking is coming up with unique solutions to solve problems, regardless of if they are Math, Science, or Engineering problems or ANY other problem you could come up with. That new building under construction? Someone had to critically think about how to keep it structurally sound and safe for its inhabitants. Critical Thinking will be extremely useful, especially if you want to pursue a career in Math, Science, Arts, or Engineering. I will reference Critical Thinking throughout this book and you should be prepared to answer the Critical Thinking Question at the start of each topic!

So what does this all have to do with Engineering? Many things, from being able to think about in-depth solutions, to knowing how to design on the computer to everything in between. I hope the methods, explanations, and diagrams throughout this book prove to be helpful. Remember: You are the engineer!

Part 1: Line Conventions & Lines

Chapter 1: What is a Line Convention?

Critical Thinking Question: Why is it important to understand Line Conventions?

So you want to know about Line Conventions? Awesome! Before you can understand Line Conventions, you must know what the definition of Line Conventions:

Line Conventions- Standardization of lines used on technical drawings by line weight and style.

The definition of Line Conventions may be a tad confusing but it will become clear before the end of the first part of this book, I promise! To put it into simpler terms, Line Conventions is a process of making lines standard on technical drawings by the thickness or look of the line. Once again, it may sound confusing, but you will understand it in due time. You will notice over the next few pages that we will begin talking about characteristics of lines and different types of lines. Some other concepts you should understand include line weight, height, depth, and shape. Shape will be important, especially during the second part of the book about Sketching.

8.

Let's consult the diagram below for a better look at shape:

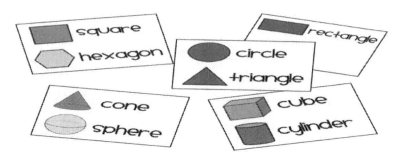

The shapes above are both 2-D and 3-D. Shape is an extremely important concept in Geometry, Sketching, and C.A.D.! Now when it comes to dealing with Line Conventions, shapes will play a role. That role is to be what the lines are forming and what it will become! Line Conventions will become a breeze by the time the first part of this book is over, that you can guarantee.

    Let's critically think for a moment: What is the big picture from dealing with Line Conventions? What can I learn? Why should I learn it? These are some questions you should try to think about for a moment. From this point on, you should consider Line Conventions to be extremely important.

    Just as a final note for now on Line Conventions, you should always follow the two "rules" mentioned earlier; line weight and line style. If you can follow the two "rules" you will be able to produce great sketches and more importantly you will understand the concepts of Line Conventions.

Chapter 2: Many Types of Lines

Critical Thinking Question: What are the different line types and how do I use them?

Now that you have a background with Line Conventions, I bet you think you're ready to sketch that design! WRONG!!! You still have a lot to learn before we can work with C.A.D. or even a freehand sketch. There are many different steps we must take to get to the point of sketching, including learning about the different types of lines!

The first thing we should ask ourselves, what is a line?

Are the figures on the next page lines? Yes! The chart is made up of many lines. The above chart is known as a "Line Graph" which is used in mathematics, science, technology, and of course engineering. The Line Graph symbolizes lines being used in real-world situations

10.

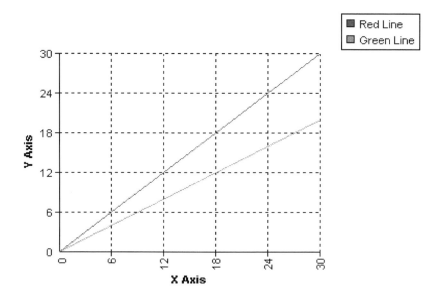

Although in this situation of the Line Graph, what the lines stand for is undefined as the information given says "Red Line" and "Green Line".

Ultimately, you're probably thinking along the lines of, "Who cares about that dumb graph, it probably doesn't represent everything." The reason why your thoughts are like that is because you are not Critically Thinking. When you think critically you think in a whole new dimension, you think out of the box, you think imaginatively and so on and so forth. We could give these lines values, for example; "Red Line" could represent... "Ice-cream Sales in the summer" while the "Green Line" could represent... "Ice-cream Sales in the winter". With that information plugged in, you can now state that Ice-cream sales are more profitable in the summer than winter.

Lines are all around us; your shoe-laces are lines, your power cords, your pencils, your pens, your chairs, everything is a line technically speaking. Why and how is that possible? The

11.

answer is because someone designed these objects to be or have lines within them. In this part of the book, you will learn about many types of lines in engineering, which will help develop your skills and prepare you for advanced sketching techniques and courses. Let's begin with Center Lines, shall we?

Chapter 3: Center Lines

Critical Thinking Question: Why do we use Center Lines?

We're going to begin by thinking round... think circular... think spherical... think half-circle... Do you know what Center Lines deal with?

Center Line- A line which defines the center of arcs, circles, or symmetrical parts.

So let's critically think again, shall we? Take the diagram below, for example:

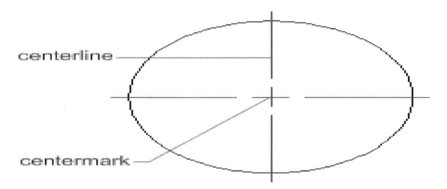

Can you tell where the Center Line is? Great, but what is that other word, Center Mark?

Center Mark- Shows the center of the circle, arc, or symmetrical parts.

13.

    Awesome! I think you're getting the hang of Center Lines, let's move into our next exciting topic: Construction Lines!

14.

Chapter 4: Construction Lines

Critical Thinking Question: How can we use Construction Lines to our advantage?

We know a lot about lines already. They're everywhere and everything around us, and we need to respect that some are longer, shorter, thicker, thinner, and so-on-and-so-forth. But the next type of line we will learn about really isn't a line by itself; by that I mean it doesn't really advocate for itself. What advocating for itself means is that the line doesn't really help itself, instead it helps other lines.

Let's add another word to our engineering and line vocabulary, shall we?

Construction Line- Lightly drawn lines to guide drawing other lines and shapes.

Guess what time it is? Time to critically think! Can you spot all the Construction Lines in the pictorial representation of the rose below?

15.

When you've found all of the Construction Lines, ask yourself why are they placed there? When you're done, let's keep moving along.

Chapter 5: Dimension Lines

Critical Thinking Question: Why do designers use Dimension Lines while sketching?

This next topic is one of the most important topics you will learn about in this book, mathematics, science, technology, and especially engineering. I bet you're already wondering, why is it so important? I'll be glad to answer that after we go over the definition of Dimension Lines. The Dimension Line definition is so confusing, you might not even be able to process it, so are you ready to learn all about Dimension Lines? No turning back now, here is the definition of a Dimension Line!

Dimension Line- A line which represents distance.

Now, I don't know if you can tell but it's a very simple definition; and yes I fooled you in the paragraph before. Dimension Lines are like the father of all Design & Modeling + I.E.D. curriculum's because they are so important to the project, just as a father is involved in bringing a newborn child into the world; but that is a different story. But did you know, real engineers have to use dimension lines as well?

Let's think for a moment, critically if you will. The lines that you see with arrows (→ and ←) and numbers in the middle on a sketch are considered dimensions. Why are they considered dimensions? One thing to keep in mind when adding dimension lines, are units. Units include, but are not limited to cm., in., ft., mm., and once again so-on-and-so-forth.

17.

    Now that you think you've got a grip on Dimension Lines, keep this in mind: Dimension Lines and Dimensioning will come back later, this is not the last time you'll hear from those two concepts. Now then, let's march ahead!

Chapter 6: Extension Lines

Critical Thinking Question: Why do we use arrows to represent Extension Lines?

The boss loves the sketch you came up with. You're all joyful inside, but wait... The boss informs you that there's been a problem with the machinery. You ask what is wrong, and he says it's a mechanical issue due to the sketch you created. You claim to have put in Dimension Lines, but it seems to not be convincing him; he responds with the following answer: Where are your Extension Lines?

I just love real-world problems connections, don't you? That scenario listed in the beginning of this chapter could really have happened, as even an engineer makes silly mistakes, such as forgetting their drawings' Extension Lines. What exactly is an Extension Line, I'm glad you asked!

Extension Line- Line which represents where a dimension starts and stops.

Now ladies and gentlemen, let's dive deeper into thought with a critical thinking challenge. When working with a Technical Drawing, we need Dimension Lines; part of having Dimension Lines is the need for Extension Lines. Think you can figure out what the Extension Lines look like? If you need a hint, refer to the Technical Drawing below:

19.

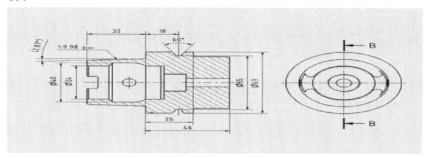

Most drawings you see in will be this detailed, so keep it in mind.

Technical Drawings can be interpreted in many ways, however you should always keep your Dimension Lines and Extension Lines easy to see and find. If they are not present, you will not get the credit you so rightfully deserve! But more importantly, if you were an engineer and you forgot your Dimension Lines and Extension Lines... oh boy I would feel so sorry for you. As mentioned in the beginning of this chapter, if your Extension Lines are missing, you will not be able to produce the part or the machine will malfunction as you did not show where the dimension was or what the units were.

To keep your mind refreshed, you should always think about Dimension Lines when dealing with Extension Lines. Why should you think about Dimension Lines? Simply because you will have to draw the arrows to represent the distance and show where that distance begins and ends. It's very important you keep your mind refreshed with the concepts because they will always come back in engineering, sketching, even art!

We will now begin to introduce some more lines that will help you understand sketching a lot more. Care to join me?

Chapter 7: Hidden Lines

Critical Thinking Question: Why are Hidden Lines important to the entire sketch?

So we're moving from hard, to harder. Great. You're probably wondering why we're jumping from one extreme to the next, the answer is to better prepare you for all the things you'll see in real-world engineering. Engineering is all about variety, as there are many different types of engineers and various fields for almost any interest. Let's chat about engineering later and keep going with the lines!

Our next "friend" is called a Hidden Line. Now you might be thinking, "Are Hidden Lines hidden?" We'll answer that... right now!

Hidden Line- A line type that represents an edge that is not directly visible.

With that definition in mind, we can translate it to easier terms: A Hidden Line is a line style that represents an edge that you can't directly see. It's much easier to remember if you put the definitions into your own words. It's also been proven that you're more likely to remember things if you put them in your own words, so you'd better be taking notes! Hidden Lines are very important as they show edges that are not easy to see and where those edges are located.

Let's critically think about a solution to a problem, shall we? If the skyscraper is 300 ft. (length) and 200 ft. (width), can you find the edge? Hmm. With the Hidden Line, we most certainly can find the solution; though you will need to sketch out your solution to the problem.

21.

We will now keep it moving with more line types, and soon you will have the skills you need to create a sketch! Let's keep it moving!

Chapter 8: Leader Lines

Critical Thinking Question: What is an arc in regards to Geometry?

    You walked into work one morning after the incident with the Extension Lines, feeling confident that your work is done correctly this time. You have all the Dimension Lines, Extension Lines, Dimensions, and Drawings complete. Uh oh, here comes the boss, and he looks unhappy already; you can tell this will not be a good situation. He says that you botched up another sketch, but when he says that you begin thinking that you did nothing wrong. You explain that you have the Drawings, Dimension Lines, Extension Lines, and Dimensions all in place and that nothing is wrong. He turns to you and asks about your arcs, circles, and small details; to which you reply in a confused tone: What is an arc?

    These connections are great, don't you agree? If I were the boss, I would have fired that man or woman a long time ago, mainly because he or she is not doing the full extent of the job. Regardless, let's discuss the next type of line, which is dubbed as the Leader Line. Let's define it!

Leader Line- Line which indicates dimensions of arcs, circles, and detail.

    Now one word you could use to go along with Leader Lines would be Line Weight. Line Weight, which was mentioned earlier; deals with the thickness of a line and it is characterized as thick or thin. The diagram on the next page shows the use of Leader Lines, can you find them?

23.

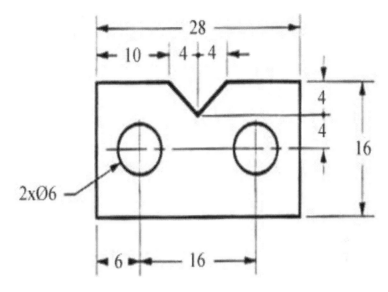

It's critical thinking time, huzzah! Using the above diagram, can you identify the radius? Remember, radius deals with circles and not squares, rectangles, triangles, perpendicular lines, parallel lines, nor hexagons; only circles. When you've found the radius, you will be able to find things such as the volume of the figure for example. As a bonus, find the volume of the figure above using volume formulas!

We're running right on schedule; soon you'll be a line and geometry master! All aboard, next stop, Long-Break Lines!

Chapter 9: Long-Break Lines

Critical Thinking Question: What do objects with "Uniform Details" look like?

"Sir, you're out of uniform." "How am I out of uniform, I'm wearing my Dimension Lines, Extension Lines, Shapes, and Details!" "Let me inspect your uniform, would you mind stepping to the side please?" "Sure, but I can't wait to rub it in that the Sketch Inspector made a mistake." "Aha! I knew I was right!" "What's wrong?" "Your Details are not in proper uniform, I'm going have to send you to your new home: the trashcan."

I wish my drawings talked like the ones you just read about. Sketches and Drawings must have something called "Uniform Details" in order to be considered a "good" or "valid" sketch. You're probably thinking, "What do Uniform Details have to do with Long-Break Lines?" Since you asked so kindly...

Long-Break Line- A line which indicates that a very long object with uniform detail is drawn foreshortened.

I spy with my little eye... a critical thinking challenge! Take a look at the previous diagrams in the book, how many Long-Break Lines can you identify in total? When you find how many, where are they located? What details do you notice?

Well, we're running, "Around The World in 13 Chapters!" Trust me, we're almost at the border of sketching and lines. You should never give up, especially when you're this close to successful drawing techniques!

25.

Chapter 10: Object Lines

Critical Thinking Question: Why should I use solid lines when sketching?

Engineers love to solve problems! Let's take a car for example, it's not running correctly, what do you do? Do you check the fuel tank? The gauges and meters inside the car? Or do you check under the hood? All of the given methods are ways to solve a problem and engineers love to solve problems! Engineers must solve everyday problems in new, innovative ways! But regardless, let's check in on our friend the worker (who I'm amazed still isn't fired, must be some extremely forgiving boss!) and see what misfortune has happened to him or her. Shall we?

The worker was ecstatic. He or she (we still don't know which) had an excellent night's sleep, and a vision for a new invention! He or she was in a rush to go send the sketch to the manufacturing department to get it out onto the market (what the invention is, I have no idea.) and make major money for the company! Before that however, the person wants to take it to the boss to be approved. The boss said to come in, and the worker shows him the sketch and he says: "Where's all the details? Where are the Object Lines?" The worker says they will do better next time, and leaves the room with a fire warning.

Oh man, this worker can't get a break! Well, he or she might get fired; I guess we'll just have to check in again soon! What the boss' complaint was this time is that there were no Object Lines!

Object Line- A heavy solid line used on a drawing to represent the outline of an object.

26.

It's a bird.... It's a plane.... No! It's a critical thinking challenge! Let's see.... I have an excellent task: What makes this sketch realistic?

Soon, you'll be a Line and Line Convention Master! I hope that you have a strong understanding of the past concepts and this one. We're more than halfway there, keep it up!

Chapter 11: Projection Lines

Critical Thinking Question: Why is it important to project views in an Orthographic Sketch?

You're doing an amazing job! I'm very impressed with how close you are to becoming a Line and Line Conventions Master! This third-to-last part of Part 1 of the book is extremely important!!!!! Please pay attention as this will help you so much when it comes to being able to sketch many different views and presenting your work! This section, by far will help you probably even more than all the other lines (with the exception of the Dimension Lines) combined! Projection Lines will help the person creating the product know what-goes-where. Let's dive deeper with a definition...

Projection Line- An imaginary line that is used to locate or project the corners, edges, and features of a three-dimensional object onto an imaginary two-dimensional surface.

Wow... that's rather confusing wouldn't you say? Let's consult a sketch for assistance...

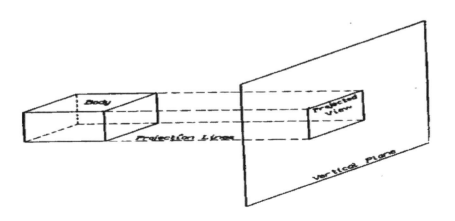

The sketch above proves the point very efficiently and simply. Simply put, Projection Lines show how and where the sketch connects to another piece or view. Let's talk though... I wouldn't want you to mess up on a sketch!

How can you be sure you're projecting correctly? The sketch shown on the previously sketch is partially accurate. The lines are projected left-to-right which is fine. However, the names of the views are incorrect; none of the views are technically called "Body" or "Vertical Plane". You should also not have to say "Projected View" as the sketcher for that drawing did, it should be; in all honesty very easy to tell it's being projected.

I'm throwing a real curve-ball into this critical thinking challenge! For this critical thinking challenge, brainstorm a solution to a problem, and sketch out the solution you came up with. It should be difficult, but don't get discouraged it is after all, your own idea and nobody can read minds, right?!

With all of this information to take in and process, I think we should take a moment to stop and think. When you've had your moment to process, head over to the second-to-last chapter about Lines and Line Conventions.

Chapter 12: Section Lines

Critical Thinking Question: Why do we need to show where to cut the figure?

The cutting board... an important place. Oh, you meant cutting parts for a certain invention-type thing? Why didn't you say so! This next type of line is really handy when it comes to dealing with cutting material. You might just find yourself using this line a lot when sketching. Without further delay, let's learn about Section Lines!

Section Line- Thin lines used in a section view to indicate where the cutting plane line has cut through material.

So what does that mean? Material is what the item is made of, so that means it shows where the item's contents have been cut. We can figure out where the material has been cut by simply looking for a specific line in the sketch. Something similar to what's shown on the diagram below:

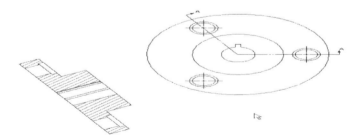

30.

Your mission, should you choose to accept it is to critically think to find a solution to this problem. This message will self-destruct in 2000 years. Can you find the Section Lines in the diagram above? If so, what figure(s) is or are the Section Lines cutting through? Ladies and Gentlemen, let's move on.

Chapter 13: Short-Break Lines

Critical Thinking Question: How can I make a part shorter?

I don't know how you did it, but you did! Congratulations on making it this far! You've learned so much about Lines and Line Conventions, you're practically a pro! We just have one more line to talk about before you can "graduate" into the next level: sketching! Short-Break Lines and then we will finish our story of the worker and his or her boss...

Short-Break Line- Line which shows where the part is broken to reveal detail behind the part or to shorten a long continuous part.

The boss had finally come up with an idea to solve the worker's forgetfulness problem... "You will write down all of your ideas, every day, every time, everything." The worker nodded in agreement to the plan. "Every time you finish a sketch, bring it to me so I can evaluate it and tell you whether or not it needs that certain something. That way, you save your job; and I make money!" The worker bounced around in delight and said before leaving the room, "Does that mean I get that raise we discussed?" The boss screamed with anger, and from that moment on the worker never had a problem with his or her job again. The End.

Wow! We can learn a lot from our mistakes and the misfortune of others, to the point where we as engineers can avoid making the same mistakes and be able to make a nice sum of money. Everything counts, and if you put your effort into something, there's no doubt you can't do it.

The final critical thinking challenge for this section is to sketch your own drawing with a Short-Break Line! Good luck!

32.

You've done it! Congratulations! You really know your stuff, and you've proven that you're worthy to learn about sketching. Good Luck, you'll need it!

Part 2: Sketching

Chapter 14: What is Sketching?

Critical Thinking Question: Why do engineers use sketching in the Design Process?

Welcome back! You've learned about the wonderful world of lines, but now we're going to kick it up a notch. Yes my friends, we will now begin talking about Sketching! Before one can sketch, you must know what a sketch is, yes? I thought so. Let's begin by learning what the definition of a sketch is.

Sketch- A rough representation of the main features of an object or scene and often made as a preliminary study.

To put that in plain English, that means its a first draft of the major parts of a thing or scene and it's usually the first stage of drawing. Sketches have actually been seen throughout this book to be honest, you can find many examples of them in Part 1 and you will continue to find sketches until this part is over as Part 3 is a Multiple Choice Test. So how do sketches (which seem more like art) relate to engineering?

The answer is simple really... The process of designing things is known as the Design Process. In most school programs we use a 12-Step Design Process, but even in real-world engineering the 12-Step Design Process exists; just simplified.

35.

The critical thinking challenges are now more difficult than before. You will receive a problem or a question, and you'll be on your own. Here is the first sketching question: What Step(s) from the 12-Step Engineering Design Process does sketching fall under?

Good luck figuring out the answer!

So now you've got a basic understanding of the 12-Step Engineering Design Process, you can do almost anything (well, we're pretty sure you can't fly.) as well as sketching. That's fine and dandy, but how do we put it to use? How does this relate to Lines and Line Conventions? Read on to discover these answers and more.

Chapter 15: Sketching and Lines Are a Perfect Pair

Critical Thinking Question: What is the relationship between a sketch and lines?

Sketching and Lines are very important to an engineer. It's also important in mathematics, science, technology, and art. But just how are they related? Lines are used to create the sketch! Without lines, there wouldn't be a sketch for the engineer to create! Is that the secret formula to a sketch, lines? I think we need to make a connection!

You're an engineer at MOCME (a fictional company) and you're designing a new juicer. You need to figure out how you will sketch the new juicer so it can be produced correctly (remember, engineers communicate in writing, drawing, sketching, and verbally; an engineer or machine cannot make a product off of what is said) without errors. So you decide to make your design really elaborate and fancy, but that's in your head; not on the paper. So how can you do it on the paper? You can use different types of lines (as described in Part 1) to create your sketch which can then turn into a drawing, which could then turn into a product!

Drawing- A formal graphical representation of an object containing information based on the drawing type.

Here's a small flowchart about the life of a sketch:

Sketch → Drawing → C.A.D. → Approval Process → Production

Let's think, critically if you will. Try to explain the following question: How does a Sketch turn into a Drawing? Tricky isn't it?

37.

    Now we shall begin talking about some basics of Sketching. Come along, there's much still to see and learn! We must get you ready for the big test at the end of the book, come on!

Chapter 16: Cabinet Pictorial

Critical Thinking Question: What is Depth?

I love to make real-world connections (as you can probably tell by now) so let's connect to a situation dealing with an engineer and drawing, shall we?

You're working on your newest drawing, it was just approved by the sketching department at MOCME (the fictional company mentioned previously) and it now is being worked on as a drawing, by you. You're adding dimensions for height and width, which is fine and dandy but you think something is missing. Your boss walks in (shocker) and says "Whoa, that's an excellent drawing; it has dimensions and the whole package of what I'm looking for!" He's ready to sign a contract to have the product made until he notices something wrong with the product. "Where's the depth to your drawing, you can't be missing the depth it's extremely important to the whole concept!" You leave the office with a pink slip and go home to cry, while your former boss signs a contract for the same product you designed; but with depth added to it.

Tough break right? Unfortunately, situations like that are common in the world of engineering; you have to be precise if you want to get your product approved. Speaking of depth, just what the heck is it, and why do engineers have to use it? There are four, count them four words you must understand for Cabinet and Cavalier Pictorials. You will learn two of them now:

Cabinet Pictorial- Oblique pictorial where depth is represented as half scale compared to the height and width scale.

Depth- The measurement associated with an object's front-to-back

39.

dimension or extent of something side to side.

Your critical thinking challenge this time around is to ask yourself, what does depth really mean? How can I understand depth? We're moving along; can't you feel your confidence building?

Chapter 17: Cavalier Pictorial

Critical Thinking Question: What is the difference between a full scale and a half scale?

I'm ready to jump right into this chapter, we're getting so close to being able to produce a beautiful sketch! Chapters 16-18 are mainly about Cabinet and Cavalier Pictorials along with Depth and Height. In the next chapter, you will learn about when to use the two different Pictorials. For now, let's zoom-in on Cavalier Pictorials. Here are the next two words for your engineering vocabulary!

Cavalier Pictorial- Oblique pictorial where height, width, and depth are represented at a full scale.

Height- The measurement associated with an object's top-to-bottom dimension.

So what exactly do these words mean? Let's consult the sketch below:

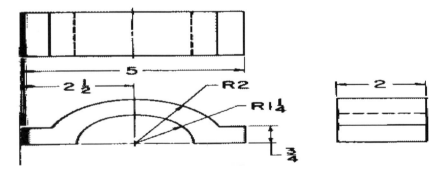

For your critical thinking challenge, can you figure out why this is

41.

a Cavalier Pictorial? If so, how can you tell?

We're certainly moving along, and that's excellent! We have a little debate to listen in on next, would you care to come? Great, let's go see the Cabinet VS. Cavalier Debate...

Chapter 18: Cabinet VS. Cavalier Pictorials

Critical Thinking Question: When should I use a Cabinet or Cavalier Pictorial?

    The big debate over Cabinet and Cavalier Pictorials began when the two types of methods to sketching came around. How can we use the two types of sketching? We will discover what they really are needed for in this chapter. But first, think about the four terms discussed while talking about pictorials (Cabinet Pictorial, Depth, Cavalier Pictorial, and Height). How do they relate to each other?

    Let's consult the following sketches to try and find the answers we seek:

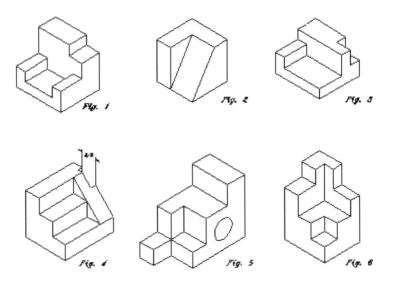

43.

What similarities are there? Half are Cabinet, the other half are Cavalier. Your challenge is to figure out which is which! Now, let's learn about the founding fathers of sketching!

Chapter 19: The Basics of Sketching: Four Major Views

Critical Thinking Question: How can I create sketches on paper and on C.A.D.?

    You're coming a long way since the beginning. You can do it, I promise! We're now going to get into the major piece of the book and sketching it: views. There are four major views used during sketching, the list is shown below with a brief description of each.

Top View- View you see when looking directly down on an object.

Front View- View you see when looking directly towards the front.

Right Side View- View you see on the right side of the figure.

Isometric View- View that all angles add up to 120 degrees.

    Now you know the four major views. Awesome. Let's see if you can now identify them in four separate sketches. Wanna test your luck? The challenge is to identify each view based off of the sketch. Good luck!

45.

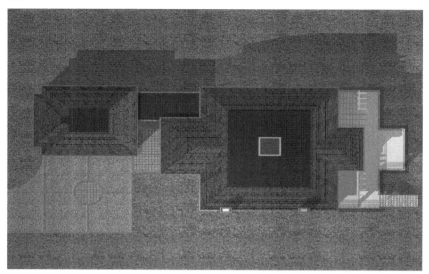

Which view is this?

A) Front, B) Right, C) Top, D) Isometric

46.

Which view is this?

A) Right, B) Front, C) Isometric, D) Top

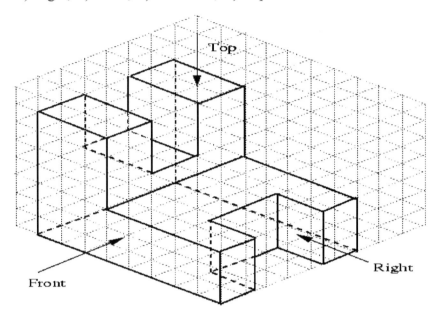

Which view is this?

A) Isometric, B) Right, C) Front, D) Top

You may have noticed that each view is there, except for the Right Side View. Why is this? It can easily be mistaken for the Left Side View, which is not a major part of the sketch. How is that possible if the Right Side View is important? To answer your question (whether you asked it or not), the Left Side View is a mirror image of the Right Side View 75% of the time or better.

Now how does this relate back to C.A.D.? Simple: C.A.D. doesn't know the views or what the sketch looks like until you create it. Sketches need to be on paper first and then transferred to a C.A.D. Software. Remember you need to understand the four basic views of sketching before you jump onto a computer and use C.A.D. Heck, it's important to know before you get your pencil and paper out! Speaking of sketches, your critical thinking challenge is to design something with the four major views, try your best and don't get discouraged!

We now will move into the last topics of the book. They are tricky to learn, but if you can do all of the previous skills I know you can do this. Come on, let's do this!

Chapter 20: One-Point Perspective: What's it All About?

Critical Thinking Question: What is the difference between "Normal" and "Parallel"?

The drawing above is a One-Point Perspective Drawing. But just what is One-Point Perspective Drawing all about? We can learn more by first understanding the definitions of Perspective, Normal, and Parallel.

Perspective- The way something is viewed, The way something is seen, How one views something, etc.

Normal- Perpendicular (only in engineering)

Parallel- Lines that are congruent (same slope)

What does all of this have to do with One-Point Perspective? Lots of things, such as: Symmetry, Slope, Geometry, Line Conventions, Sketching, and Drawing. You need to understand all of these concepts before doing One-Point Perspective or Two-Point Perspective. All of the previous topics really build to the point where you can do a One-Point or Two-Point Perspective Drawing, so do refresh yourself if you need to!

Your critical thinking challenge is to figure out why the lines are "Normal" in the drawing on the previous page. What makes the drawing a One-Point Perspective Drawing? What views are shown for this drawing? How can I draw something like this? Use those questions to guide or explain your thinking.

49.

    We're really close to the end; don't let your guard down now! We need to discuss Two-Point Perspective and then we can reflect on your work from this book! Let's do it to it!

Chapter 21: Two-Point Perspective: A Fresh Look

Critical Thinking Question: What is the difference between One-Point and Two-Point Perspective?

When dealing with sketches, we must understand that we are dealing with lines, shapes, and paper. We need to understand that the paper is our canvas, and we are preparing a masterpiece. Even if it's not what you wanted, do not ever throw your masterpiece in the trash; it will come back to bite you! We will begin to talk about Two-Point Perspective, but not in great detail. So let's begin with stating the differences between One and Two-Point Perspective.

If you noticed previously, One-Point Perspective was a Front View. But notice the drawing above, it's a combination of quite a few views. It's a combination of Isometric, Front, and Right Side View. That's three out of the four major views discussed!

If you notice, there are more details on a Two-Point Perspective Drawing, when compared to a One-Point Perspective. This is not always the case however; it's up to the designer todecide whether or not they want to put tons of detail into their drawings. Personally, I prefer the Two-Point Perspective because it seems to be more realistic and three-dimensional compared to the One-Point Perspective Drawing. But that's up to you to decide which method you prefer. As an engineer, you will have to be able understand and create both One and Two-Point Perspective Drawings.

For your next critical thinking challenge, you should create a Two-Point and a One-Point Perspective Drawing. When they're complete, put them beside each other and compare them. What makes this one different from the other? Which has more detail? Why should I care about the two different types? Does one look better than the other? Ponder those questions as you compare and work.

We've just about reached the end of our lessons! Let's move along and try to figure out where to next, come on now. I promise once again, it won't be too bad.

Chapter 22: Where to Next: A Reflection of Your Work

Critical Thinking Questions: How can I go the "Extra Mile"?

What can I learn from this book?

Wow, I can't believe we're at the end already! You've come quite a long way since you opened the cover of this book. I have to say I'm very impressed with how much you've learned, as well as how much you've done. I hope by now you understand the major concepts from this book about Lines and Sketching if not, I hope you'll go back and refresh your memory. One part of being an engineering student is being able to reflect on your work, which is what we will do now.

From the moment you picked up this book, you probably thought this was going to boring. This book was not created to entertain you nor to make you chuckle, but to indulge your mind in a new innovative way. This is one of the reasons why I love being an ESUMS student, I get to help others and come up with innovative and imaginative solutions to problems. However, you might not be from ESUMS; in fact you might just be someone looking to brush up on your sketching skills or you want to become an engineer. There are so many possibilities I won't even listen them all because there's too many!

53.

In Part 1 you learned about Lines and Line Conventions. From Construction Lines to Short-Break Lines you learned it all (I hope). We made connections to real-world issues, such as the story of the boss and his worker who kept messing up. Throughout Part 1 you learned many new things in what I hope was a fun and innovative way, and I hope it also helped you imagine new things and opened your mind to new possibilities.

Shortly after Part 1, Part 2 rolled around. In Part 2, you learned about Sketches, Drawings, Views, Perspective Drawing, and a whole bunch of great topics. These are the fundamentals to all designing in engineering and even in art. So Part 2 was designed to make sure you understood the concepts in Part 1, while adding new concepts to expand your academic vocabulary and skills as a future engineer. In Part 2, you also learned about the 12-Step Engineering Design Process (PLTW) and why it's critical when it comes to engineering and design.

One of the unique parts to this book in my opinion, is that each chapter had a Critical Thinking Question which was designed to help guide your thinking as you read. This chapter has two Critical Thinking Questions because this is the final chapter and your reflection. Another unique part to this book was that each chapter had a Critical Thinking Challenge built into it, hopefully you attempted a few of them. Go back and try them again after reading the entire book, the change in results may surprise you.

Overall, I hope you have enjoyed reading the book and I want to be the first to congratulate you on completing the first steps to becoming an engineer. You truly have come a long way, regardless of if people say the book was short or boring or whatever the case may be. I truly put a lot of effort into making the final product and hope you have had some fun and learned a lot throughout the course of the book.

54.

You truly are the engineer! Congratulations! Good Luck on Part 3, which is the "Test Your Knowledge" test! Thanks again for reading!

-Daniel Molster

Part 3:
Test Your Knowledge

Directions: There are 5 questions on this Post-Assessment. Each topic has been covered in the book. There are two Multiple Choice and three Open-Ended Response Questions.

Write all answers on a separate sheet of paper. Check your answers on the page after the test.

Good Luck, future engineers!

57.

1. What is Engineering?

A. Making stuff

B. Imagining, Investigating, and Inventing

C. Problem-Solving and Critically Thinking

D. All of the Above

2. Why do Engineers use Line Conventions?

3. Why do Engineers sketch?

4. How many steps are in the Engineering Design Process?

A. 40

B. 10

C. 2

D. 12

5. What do Lines mean to Engineers?

Answer Key

Directions for use: Self-Check your answers, if Open-Ended are similar then it is right.

1. D.

2. Engineers use Line Conventions for Technical Drawings and in everyday situations.

3. Engineers sketch to give a first thought when designing different products.

4. D.

5. Lines, to Engineers mean sketches, drawings, and everyday critical thinking and problem-solving.

About the Author

Daniel Molster is a 14 year old who currently attends the Engineering and Science University Magnet School (ESUMS). He has been a student at ESUMS since 6th Grade and is currently in 9th Grade taking the I.E.D. Engineering Course. His passions are using computers, helping others, and playing with his dog, Buddy. He hopes to become a great teacher someday in English, History, or Science.

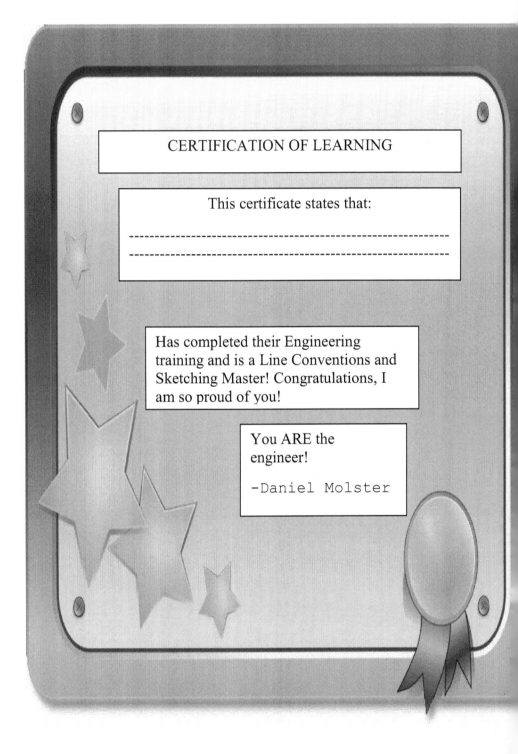

Made in the USA
Charleston, SC
05 November 2013